A Rookie reader®

You Say Hola, I Say Hello

Written by
Elizabeth Zapata

Illustrated by
Cathy Ann Johnson

To Zoë and Maya, *mi Tizón y mi Rubia*, and to my Bonfire, I love you
— E.Z.

For my wonderful nieces
— C.A.J.

Consultant

Eileen Robinson
Reading Specialist

Library of Congress Cataloging-in-Publication Data

Zapata, Elizabeth, 1973-
You say hola, I say hello / written by Elizabeth Zapata ; illustrated by Cathy Ann Johnson.
    p. cm. — (A rookie reader)
  Summary: Two friends, one who speaks English and one who speaks Spanish, contrast various words in their respective languages.
  ISBN 0-516-24859-6 (lib. bdg.)   0-516-25018-3 (pbk.)
  [1. Spanish language—Fiction. 2. Friendship—Fiction.] I. Johnson, Cathy Ann, 1964- ill. II. Title. III. Series.

PZ7.Z25683Yo 2005
[E]—dc22
                                        2004030158

CHILDREN'S PRESS, and A ROOKIE READER®, and associated logos are trademarks and or registered trademarks of Scholastic Library Publishing. SCHOLASTIC and associated logos are trademarks and or registered trademarks of Scholastic Inc.
1 2 3 4 5 6 7 8 9 10 R 14 13 12 11 10 09 08 07 06 05

You say ¡Hola!
I say hello!

You say mamá.

I say mommy.

You say hermano.
I say brother.

You say casa.
I say home.

You say escuela.
I say school.

11

You say maestro.

I say teacher.

You say libros.
I say books.

You say sol.
I say Sun.

You say perro.
I say dog.

19

You say luna.
I say moon.

21

You say adiós.
I say good-bye.

23

Word List (25 words)

(Words in **bold** are story words that are repeated throughout the text.)

English Words		Spanish Words	
books	mommy	adiós	maestro
brother	moon	casa	mamá
dog	**say**	escuela	perro
good-bye	school	hermano	sol
hello	Sun	hola	
home	teacher	libros	
I	**you**	luna	

About the Author

Elizabeth Zapata is a second-generation Puerto Rican from Bronx, New York. Learning the Spanish language is what has helped her become who she is today and she is forever thankful to have been able to inherit the culture and the love of the language from her mother. She plans to pass this gift to her daughter Zoë.

About the Illustrator

Cathy Ann Johnson is a graduate of Columbus College of Arts and Design. When Cathy isn't painting, she enjoys shopping for antiques, studying different languages, and playing her guitar.